C000284720

The People's Hi

Penshaw, Shiney Row, Philadelphia & Newbottle

by

Lena Cooper

Previous page: Residents of Quarry Head, Shiney Row, *circa* 1912.

Copyright © Lena Cooper 2000

First published in 2000 by

The People's History Ltd
Suite 1
Byron House
Seaham Grange Business Park
Seaham
Co. Durham
SR7 0PY

ISBN 1 902527 31 3

No part of this publication may be reproduced, stored in a mechanical retrieval system, or transmitted, in any form or by any means, electronic, mechanical, photocopying, recording or otherwise, without prior permission of the author.

Contents

Lena Cooper dedicates this book to the memory of Norman Curry Cooper and to the memory of Maureen Lilian Cooper.

Introduction

The villages around Penshaw Monument are of particular interest to me, especially Penshaw, where I spent a number of years. Even when I moved away to other places, part of my heart remained there – it will always be very special to me.

Remembering how things were will, I'm sure, bring back some wonderful nostalgic memories of the mining and agricultural backgrounds of Cox Green, Penshaw, Shiney Row, Herrington Burn, Philadelphia and Newbottle. Last but most important – the wonderful people of the villages – I salute them! Enjoy the book.

Lena Cooper

Shiney Row looking towards Herrington Burn from Chester Road, *circa* 1915. T. Cox & Sons, general dealers, is on the front left and Beatrice Terrace is on the right.

Acknowledgements

Lena Cooper acknowledges with grateful thanks the following people for their contribution of photographs and/or stories towards the compilation of this book:

Mr G. Atkinson, Mr Derek Beattie, Mrs Molly Beattie, Miss Dawn Cummings, Mrs Ena Curry, Mr Malcolm Eves, Mrs Hilda English, Mrs Mary Hagley, Mr Morgan Hardy, Mr Stephen Watson Hardy, Headteachers of Barnwell Primary School, Penshaw; New Penshaw Primary School; Our Lady Queen of Peace RC School, Penshaw; Shiney Row Primary School and Newbottle Primary School, Councillor John Mawston, JP, ISM, Mr Alan Oliver, Mr J. Osman, Mrs Pat Patterson, Mr & Mrs A. Warren and Mr Alan Yardley.

Special thanks are also due to:

Mr Andrew Clark and Mr George Nairn whose help and encouragement kept me going.

Appreciation and thanks for co-operation go to:

Lord Joicey
Beamish Archives – The North of England Open Air Museum
Alan Rutter
The YMCA – Herrington Burn
Northeast Press Limited, Sunderland Echo

Bibliography

Michael Bute *A Town Like Alice's*
Tom Corfe & Geoffrey Milburn *Buildings and Beliefs*
Dawn Cummings *Penshaw – The History of a Village*
Norman Emery *Banners of the Durham Coalfield*
Stuart Miller *Something For You From Sunderland*
Stuart Miller & George Nairn *Around Washington*
Ken Richardson *Houghton-le-Spring and Hetton-le-Hole in Old Photographs*
Ken Richardson *Houghton-le-Spring and Hetton-le-Hole in Old Photographs – A Second Selection*
Shiney Row Local History Society *Shiney Row Remembered*
S.A Staddon *The Tramways of Sunderland*

Kelly's Directories of Durham and Northumberland

COX GREEN AND PENSHAW

The boathouse viewed from the Cox Green side of the River Wear.

Cox Green village, *circa* 1947. In the distance can be seen Washington Chemical Works, Coke Works and Brickworks on the other side of the River Wear.

The ferry at Cox Green in the early 1950s.

Victoria Bridge with Low Lambton ferry to 'Butney' Pit (North Biddick Colliery).

The bridge from Cox Green to Washington Chemical Works. The bridge was opened in 1958 to replace the ferry.

Low Lambton, *circa* 1940s. A small group of houses since demolished.

A group of men with children and dogs outside the Oddfellows Arms, Cox Green, in the early 1900s. Note most of the men appear to be pipesmokers.

A passenger train standing in Cox Green Railway Station, *circa* 1960s. The station was closed to passengers in 1964.

Rebuilt in 1895, Alice Well at Cox Green was the only source of water up to 1947. The well is thought by some to have helped inspire Lewis Carroll in his books *Alice's Adventures in Wonderland* and *Through the Looking Glass*. Carroll (Charles Lutwidge Dodgson) was a regular visitor to the area in the nineteenth century.

Cox Green village viewed from the Washington side of the bridge in 1958. Note Penshaw Monument in the background.

Washington Chemical Works viewed from the Cox Green side of the bridge in the late 1950s. The chemical works have long since gone and the land reclaimed for new industries and a housing estate.

The ferry at Cox Green. Kelly's Directory of 1921 included a total of nine commercial entries for Cox Green: John Allan, shopkeeper; Mrs Sarah Ann Bradley, farmer; Church Institute (secretary William Clark); Thomas Curtis, Oddfellows' Arms; Thomas Harrison, confectioner; Horn & Scott, quarry owners; John McMenam, Royal William inn; John Robinson, shopkeeper and Wearside Golf Club (hon secretary Hartley French).

A view of the River Wear near Washington with the village of Cox Green on the left.

A view of Penshaw Monument from Cox Green. The foundation stone for Penshaw's most famous landmark was laid on 28th August 1844. It was dedicated to John George Lambton, first Earl of Durham who had died four years previously. The design was based on the Theseum in Athens, although, Penshaw's version is smaller with 18 columns as opposed to 54. The £6,000 building costs was raised by public subscription.

Residents at the Bore Hole, *circa* 1900.

The farmhouse of North Farm, Cox Green, *circa* 1909.

The Wearside Golf Club, Cox Green.

A view of Gladstone Terrace leading down to Fatfield Bridge taken from the bridge at New Penshaw Station.

Penshaw village, 1913, showing from the left: All Saints Church, the Grey Horse Inn, T&R Bird (cash grocers) and the Ship Inn (now renamed The Monument).

A postcard of Old Pensher in the early 1900s. Note the old spelling. The population of Penshaw in 1901 was 3,777, in the next decade the population soared to 6,431.

A general view of Penshaw Railway Station and signal box, *circa* 1950.

Penshaw Railway Station, *circa* 1950s. In the early part of the twentieth century the station was on Bishop Auckland and Penshaw branch of the North East railway. The Penshaw station master during the First World War was one Frederick Yarrow Watson.

Penshaw War Memorial, *circa* 1920. The names of the fallen from the Second World War were added to the Memorial later.

Gladstone Terrace, New Penshaw, *circa* 1936.

An earlier view of Gladstone Terrace, New Penshaw in the late 1920s.

Rose Street West, Old Penshaw, *circa* 1914. Single cottages on the left and Rose Street East – 'up and downers' – on the right. In those days most streets had a corner shop.

Rose Street East, Old Penshaw, had a drapery shop in the centre of the street and a general dealer's shop at the end in the 1930s. Note the milk float in the centre. Milk was delivered from the farms direct to the door and measured out in gills, pints or quarts by the milkman.

Chester Road, Penshaw, *circa* 1907. The top of Penshaw Monument can just be seen in the centre.

Penshaw Lane, also known as Chester Road, Penshaw, *circa* 1940.

Penshaw Lane also leads up to the church from Chester Road. Note J.E.
Thompson's general dealer shop front left, *circa* 1914.

Penshaw North Farm milk float in Rose Street West, *circa* 1940s.

Local schoolchildren celebrating the 'Festival of Trees' within the pillars of Penshaw Monument in 1993.

Restoration of Penshaw Monument in 1979. At one time you could walk round the top of the monument, gaining access through a spiral staircase in one of the columns. This was stopped after the death of a 16-year-old Fatfield boy who fell from the top in 1926.

J.W. Applegarth & Son, butchers, Penshaw. Some of Applegarth's neighbouring shops included: Frederick Petrie, artificial teeth maker; Jane Elliott, draper; Thomas Potts Stewart, grocer and James Currant Jnr, gramophone, cycle & general dealer, picture framer & photographic enlarger.

Mr and Mrs J.W. Applegarth, Penshaw.

Staff of Harry Johnson, high class pork butcher, Penshaw.

The Grey Horse Inn, Old Penshaw village. At the outbreak of the First World War Joseph Hunter Raine was landlord at the Grey Horse. Other Penshaw pubs included: Bird-in-Hand, Prospect Inn and Ship Inn. Between the wars, as well as public houses, Penshaw boasted a number of clubs. These included Comrades' Social Club (secretary Harry Barker) and North Biddick Institute (secretary George Richardson).

The Prospect Inn, Old Penshaw, *circa* 1930s. The building at one time was a school house for the children of local miners.

The Ship Inn, Old Penshaw, *circa* 1930s.

Major James H. Howe MBE, LRAM, ARCM, was born on 11th November 1917 at Lambton Terrace in Penshaw. At the age off 11 he played the cornet in Shiney Row Colliery Silver Prize Band, his father being bandmaster at the time. Leaving school in 1933, a time when good jobs were hard to find, he eventually managed to be recruited to serve in the Royal Scots as a band boy. In May 1940 the Royal Scots Regiment were rushed to Belgium to help repel enemy invaders and Jimmy Howe was taken prisoner. He was sent to Stalag VIIIB near Breslau along with the medical officer, the Padre and his band sergeant. It was not long before a camp dance orchestra was formed under Jimmy Howe's direction, using instruments got through the International Red Cross and Polish POWs. Augmented by civilian musicians who were from the Territorial Army.

After demobilisation, he decided to pursue his long held ambition to become a bandmaster and in 1945 started the course of a student bandmaster at the Royal Military School of Music. In 1949 his first appointment was as bandmaster, the Argyll and Sutherland Highlanders. Then his highest hopes were achieved when 10 years later he became Director of Music of the Scots Guards. In his career he rose from band boy to Senior Director of Music of the Brigade of Guards (Household Division).

British Prisoner of War dance orchestra led by Jimmy Howe (in white suit), Stalag VIIIB, Germany in the early 1940s. The music stands, initialed J.H., were made of paper. The neat appearance of the men is due to jackets being made of fine linen material in which their captors took deliveries of tea.

An aerial view of Penshaw Monument in 1985

An aerial view of Old Penshaw village from 1985 showing All Saints Church (left of centre) and the Grey Horse Inn (centre). The Ship Inn – now renamed the Monument – is just right of centre.

SECTION TWO

SHINEY ROW

Shiney Row War Memorial.

Chester Road, Shiney Row, *circa* 1910. On the left is the United Methodist Chapel, now the site of Trinity Church, while on the right stands Long Row. This site is now occupied by Grangewood Close and Grangewood Garage. The population of Shiney Row (including Philadelphia and part of New Herrington) in 1911 was 4,174.

Quarry Head, Shiney Row, *circa* 1912. The men are standing outside the Shoulder of Mutton public house.

A general view of a street called Mill Pit, Shiney Row. On the right is the Traveller's Rest public house.

The Shiney Row branch of Newbottle and District Co-operative Society. This Co-operative Society no longer exists and the building is now used for a variety of purposes, including a bedding centre and other businesses.

Shiney Row Branch of the Chester-le-Street Co-operative Society at Boult Terrace, *circa* 1908.

L. Bylton from Shiney Row in the Royal Flying Corps uniform of the First World War. The Flying Corps had been formed in 1912 and was the predecessor of the Royal Air Force (formed April 1918).

Jane Dagless in her garden at 5 Lowerson Avenue, Shiney Row, *circa* 1940s.

Shiney Row Post Office, *circa* 1908.

Front Street, Shiney Row, *circa* 1920s. The Swan Inn is on the left and the street on the right is now known as Westbourne Terrace. At the beginning of the First World War Thomas Swinhoe ran the Swan Inn. Other pubs in Shiney Row at this time included: Travellers' Rest (William Dobson), Oddfellows' Arms (William Carr), Shoulder of Mutton (William Haddock), Londonderry Hotel (George Spoors) and Wheatsheaf (William Smith). For those who did not partake in the hard stuff there was Emmanuel Littlefair's temperance bar.

Mr & Mrs W. Inch at the door of their confectioner's shop at Shiney Row.

Mr E. Taylor of Foundry Farm, Shiney Row. This later became Denis Stark's DIY Depot.

Westbourne Terrace, Shiney Row, early 1900s. This view is before the shops as they are now. Coffin Row is on the left.

Gladdy Wilson in front of Birkbeck's shoe shop, Coffin Row, Shiney Row.

A view of Junction Row showing the Wesleyan Methodist Chapel, right of centre. Eventually it was demolished in stages. In the early twentieth century this part of County Durham was a stronghold of Methodism. Kelly's Directory of 1914 noted as well as the one at Junction Row, 'There are Wesleyan and Primitive Methodist chapels in Newbottle; Wesleyan, Primitive Methodist and United Methodist chapels in Philadelphia.'

The Oddfellows' Arms, Shiney Row.

HERRINGTON BURN
AND PHILADELPHIA

The post office, grocer and general dealer, Philadelphia.

The Electric Power Station, Philadelphia, *circa* 1920s.

The Lambton Castle Inn, Philadelphia. In 1921 Jesse Burton ran the Lambton Castle.

The Atkinson family
of Raglan Row,
Philadelphia, in the
1940s.

Mr Hunter Turnbull
at Bunker Hill
gardens.

Mr B. Lawton and his son Tom with their dog at 2 Yard Row, Philadelphia, *circa* 1940s.

Mrs Gill (née Young) and her father in their shop doorway at Shop Row, Philadelphia, *circa* 1913.

Old Herrington Burn with the Tivoli Cinema to the left background and the old YMCA building on the right, *circa* 1920s.

Miners' Homes, Herrington Burn, 1907. These were opened the previous year and were the first Aged Miners' cottages built (as opposed to converted) in County Durham.

Front Street, New Herrington, in the early 1900s. This street was on the tram route to Houghton-le-Spring.

Front Street, New Herrington, looking towards Herrington Burn in the early 1930s.

Old Herrington Burn early in the twentieth century.

A social club group of miners probably from New Herrington Colliery and the Dorothea (Dolly) Colliery, Philadelphia. The New Herrington Workingmen's Club Pavilion was their meeting place in those days.

Another group outside New Herrington Workingmen's Club Pavilion. Can any readers recognise anyone here?

Believed to be a newly delivered bus at Herrington Burn. Sunderland District Tramways began running buses in the 1920s in competition to their own trams to keep up with their rivals.

A general view of Herrington Burn. Included are the People's Profit Sharing Stores run by George Graham Ltd and a single decker bus bound for Ryhope.

Herrington Burn, *circa* 1939.

The bridge carrying the colliery railway line from Houghton Colliery to Philadelphia. The bridge has since been demolished.

Herrington Burn with the Tivoli Cinema, right centre, and bus shelter in front.

Front Street, Herrington Burn, *circa* 1930.

Grieve's Buildings, Herrington, completed in the late 1800s. The licensee of the off-licence was F.W. Black.

Railway Terrace with New Herrington Colliery in the background.

Another view of Herrington Burn showing the old YMCA building (centre) with the Tivoli Cinema on the left. Both have now been demolished.

NEWBOTTLE

Outside the Sun Inn, Newbottle, *circa* 1920s. At this time Newbottle's other pubs included: Fox and Hounds, Smiths Arms, Jolly Potters, Queen's Head, William IV, Wheatsheaf and Havelock Arms.

South Bank Lane, Newbottle.

Grasswell, showing Clifton's butcher shop, to the right of the bus, extending along to a newsagents. In the background are three rows of colliery houses at Sunniside. The foreground shows the area where Newbottle Row and Lambton Row stood before demolition.

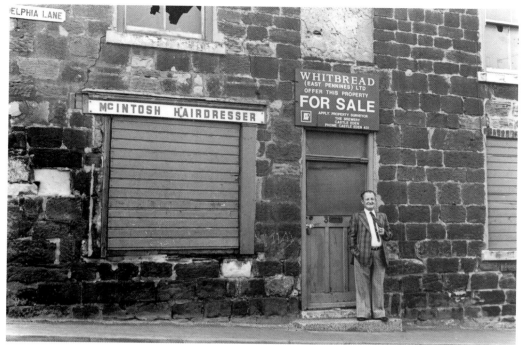

At the top of Philadelphia Lane, Newbottle, was this shop (which belonged to Mr McIntosh hairdresser). It and the adjacent buildings are now dwelling houses.

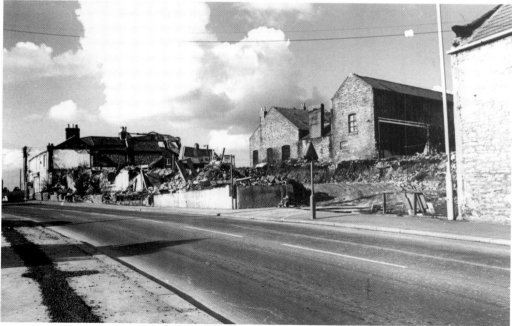

This scene was photographed from School Lane, Newbottle. The old post office is to the left and to the right is the back buildings of Newbottle Co-operative Society with recently demolished houses at the front.

The crossroads at the top of Coaley Lane, Newbottle. The shop and two houses to the left were demolished and the area is now grassed over.

Newbottle village with St Matthew's (centre background). The two front bus shelters were each vandalised and only the one on the left was rebuilt. The other was removed. The road leading off mid-left goes to Herrington Burn and Shiney Row.

The old Newbottle Co-operative Society Building was taken over by James Little, wholesale meat trader. It was then demolished and a nursing residential home built on the site.

Some of the staff of Newbottle Co-operative Society.

Staff from several departments of Newbottle Co-operative Society. The Co-operative movement began in Rochdale in 1844 when a group of weavers bought their supplies together in bulk and divided profits. Newbottle Co-operative Society was one of thousands that flourished in working class areas. One of the benefits shopping at the Co-op brought its members was a dividend. When a purchase was made your personal 'divi' number was given and a shareout was paid twice a year.

Left: Newbottle Co-operative Society's horse-drawn butcher's cart, *circa* 1930s. The driver Mr Groves was a familiar figure in the area.

Brompton Terrace, Newbottle, *circa* 1913.

Top of Front Street, Newbottle.

Front Street, Newbottle, looking towards the road leading down to Herrington Burn, *circa* 1913.

Front Street, Newbottle, *circa* 1913. A view from the opposite approach to that of the photograph above.

South Bank Lane, Newbottle, *circa* 1922.

Sunderland District Tramway at Newbottle, *circa* 1905. Local trams ran for twenty years between 1905 and 1925. Increasing competition from buses led to the closure of the District tramway system.

Houghton Road, Newbottle, in the early 1900s.

Main Front Street, Newbottle, 1979.

SCHOOLS

Mr Troup, headmaster of Cox Green School, standing in the doorway of the Mission Hall.

Barnwell Primary School reception class looking around the school in June 1989.

The recorder group of Barnwell School, Christmas 1976.

Barnwell Primary School Christmas Party, 1988.

No Christmas party is complete without Santa Claus. Barnwell Primary School, December 1988.

Above and below: Barnwell Primary School, Penshaw, 2000.

New Penshaw Primary School, 2000.

Our Lady Queen of Peace RC School, Penshaw, 2000.

Class 1 of Our Lady Queen of Peace RC Primary School, Penshaw, 1952.

Older pupils from Our Lady Queen of Peace RC Primary School, Penshaw, show off their many talents in a musical show in 1952.

PC Medd with pupils of Our Lady Queen of Peace RC Primary School showing off their Water Safety badges, received from Chief Superintendent David Lander, head of Washington Police in 1980.

Planting a tree in the grounds of Our Lady Queen of Peace RC Primary School on 10th March 1993 – the 10th anniversary of National 'No Smoking Day'. Young pupils lend a helping hand.

Book contentment! Such a happy picture I could not leave it out. The pupils are from Our Lady Queen of Peace RC Primary School, Penshaw. Does anyone know what year?

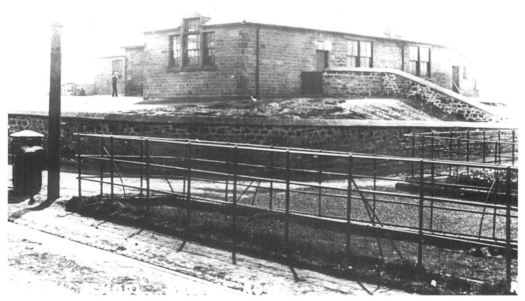

Lady Londonderry Band Hill School, Station Road, Shiney Row. The building later became the Masonic Hall.

Shiney Row Primary School.

Shiney Row School, Infants Department, Standard 1, 1920.

A class from Shiney Row Junior School in 1982.

Staff at Shiney Row Primary School in 1998. Seated, in the centre, is Mr Taylor, headteacher.

The whole of Shiney Row Primary School walk to Penshaw Monument in 1999.

Litter pickers at Shiney Row Primary School, part of the National Clean-up Campaign in 2000.

Pupils from Shiney Row Primary School enjoying a day trip to Beamish Museum.

Shiney Row Primary School, 2000.

Playground and back view of Shiney Row Primary School, 2000.

Shiney Row Nursery School in 1981.

Shiney Row Nursery dressing up as book characters in 1999.

Junction Row schoolchildren in fancy dress in 1925. Mrs Hauxwell is back left and Mrs Dixon is back right.

Paddock Stile Primary School, Philadelphia, looking towards Newbottle. The school is now demolished and other buildings occupy the site.

Paddock Stile Primary School looking down towards Herrington Burn.

Paddock Stile Junior School, Philadelphia, *circa* 1930. Note the bell-tower – a rare sight. The school was built in 1874 to cater for 307 mixed and 163 infants. In the 1920s George Oates was master and Mrs M. Betteridge the infants' mistress.

Maypole dancing at Newbottle School for the Coronation in 1953. Dancing around the maypole was a tradition maintained by local schools for many years. Empire Day was another school celebration with children showing their patriotism by waving little union jacks.

Domestic science (cookery) class at Newbottle School in May 1952. The headteacher at the time was Mr F.A. Woodley. Not a boy in sight!

Some of the staff at Newbottle Secondary School, 1968. Left to right: Derek English, Dave Taylor, Angela Tate (clerk), Edwin Gillies (headteacher), Brian Goodwin, Harry Bridges and Agnes Blanckley.

Newbottle Secondary School staff in 1968. Headteacher Mr Gillies is in the front row, third from the left.

Newbottle School prizewinners, 1951-52.

A group of pupils who received prizes at Newbottle School in the 1970s.

Demolition starts on the old Newbottle Primary School in the Spring of 1992. The school was built in 1880 but was enlarged over the years. In the 1920s Thomas J. Jeffrey was the master, Miss L. Williamson the mistress and Miss Mary Cawthorne the infants' mistress.

Newbottle schoolchildren, A. Riddell and Ian Johnston, take their music lesson seriously.

At Newbottle Primary
School refreshment time
is a happy break. Helen
Merrill and Alex Holland
think so.

Newbottle School's
younger children enjoy
their Christmas party in
1995.

Newbottle Primary School's Christmas production of 'The Animals' Story' of the Nativity in 1995.

The 'four-legged animals' masks used by the children in their Christmas production in 1995.

WORK

Penshaw 'D' Pit (or Whitefield 'D') with fan house.

New Herrington Colliery.

Railway Terrace, New Herrington.

New Herrington Colliery in the background with Railway Terrace on the left, *circa* 1900s.

A pit pony with handler at
New Herrington Colliery on
5th September 1907. The pony
had worked for 26 years in
the mine.

Workmen at Herrington
Colliery, *circa* 1920s. Front
right is Norman Turnbull.

New Herrington Colliery before closure.

A group of workmen at Philadelphia Colliery. In 1905 a special service was run by Sunderland District Tramways at 2 o'clock in the morning to take miners in the area to work. The fare was one penny and were sold in books of 12 once a fortnight when the men got paid.

A general view of Philadelphia Margaret Pit. Note the iron lattice headstock and the circular tubs on the gantry in the foreground. Perhaps they are for coke ovens or brickworks at Newbottle.

The Philadelphia Lodge Banner in the 1930s showing portraits of A.J. Cook, Peter Lee and Kier Hardie. Cook was one of the leaders of the 1926 Strike, Lee was General Secretary of the Durham Miners' Association and Keir Hardie was the first Labour MP. Of course the name of Peter Lee lives on in the town named after him.

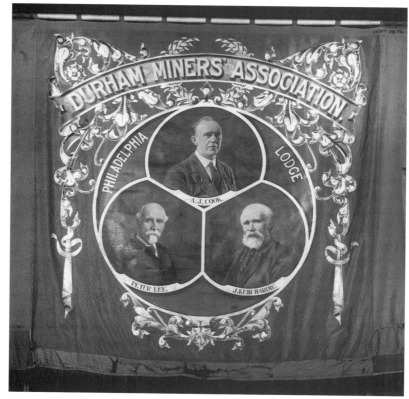

Coal hewers at
Dorothea Pit,
Philadelphia. The
Dorothea or Dolly
dated from 1816 and
did not close until
1958.

Miners outside the
lamp cabin at the
Dorothea Colliery,
circa 1930. The first
miner on the steps
with a lamp is
Stephen Watson.

Margaret and Dorothea Pits' officials at Newbottle Colliery in 1925. Fourth from the right in the back row is Arthur Garr.

The Dorothea Pit, Philadelphia.

The erectors of Lambton, Hetton & Joicey Collieries at Philadelphia in the early 1900s.

Lambton, Hetton & Joicey Collieries Locomotives at Philadelphia in the summer of 1952.

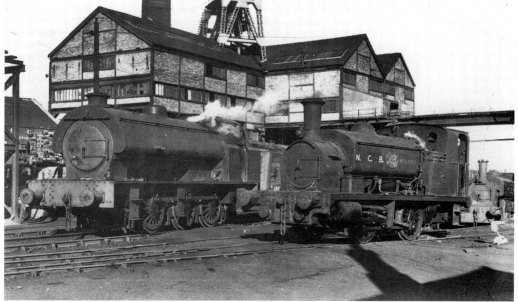

The engine shop at Philadelphia in the mid 1950s.

Councillor J.T. Hall at Philadelphia engine sheds.

Philadelphia wagon shops, 1947. Front left is Mr Lawson (manager) who is presenting Mr W. Robson with a pair of bowling shoes on his retirement. In the centre front is Mr Percy Rennie (foreman) with Tommy Greenwell (chargeman) just behind Mr Rennie.

The NCB Workshops at Philadelphia in the late 1970s. At the back right is the Central Stores.

Another view of the workshops at the Philadelphia Complex in the late 1970s.
Note Penshaw Monument in the background.

An unidentified colliery steam locomotive being cut up at Philadelphia.

An NCB steam locomotive, possibly No 29, hauling a train of coal wagons near Philadelphia.

An engine at Philadelphia for removing snow and ice from railway lines so they would be clear for the movement of locomotives.

Foundry workers at Lambton Engine Works, Philadelphia.

Sunderland District Electrical Tramway Co, car shed, Philadelphia. In his book *The Tramways of Sunderland* S.A. Staddon described how a letter addressed to 'Car Shades, Fillydelfer' was still delivered to the company.

Tram cleaners and workmen at Philadelphia tram sheds during the First World War.

Workmen of George McCall, builder, cartwright, joiner and undertaker, Penshaw. The date is thought to be before the Second World War.

Alf Hind & Son, builders, during the construction of Frederick Gardens, New Penshaw, *circa* 1930s.

A scavenger cart in Prince Street, Shiney Row, *circa* 1930. The driver is Luke Wilson.

Working with the 'trasher' (thresher) at North Farm, Cox Green.

A pony-pulled lawn mower at New Herrington.

Farmer Tindale of
Newbottle at Hopper
Square.

Fred Wylam,
confectioner, Newbottle.
At this time some of the
other shops in
Newbottle included:
Elsie Liddell,
confectioner; James
Hoggett, hairdresser;
Thomas Henderson,
fried fish dealer; John
Stokoe Hunter, grocer &
draper and William
Thompson Palmer,
grocer & fruiterer.

'Ned' Weightman's milking team at Herrington. He kept 100 cows at that time.

Fancy dress at Taylor's Farm, Shiney Row, *circa* 1920. Included are: Mrs Sparks, Mrs Kirtley, Mrs Willow (Foster) and Mrs Taylor.

CHURCH AND CHAPEL

Rogation Tide Service on Penshaw Hill Quarry, *circa* 1950. To the right is the Bishop of Manchester followed by the Reverend R. Sutton, the Rector of All Saints Church, Penshaw.

All Saints Church, Old Penshaw in the early 1900s.

The Church, Penshaw. 870

All Saints Church, Penshaw, *circa* 1900s. All Saints dates from the middle of the eighteenth century and was altered in 1876-77 at a cost of £2,000.

All Saints Church, Old Penshaw, *circa* 1930.

All Saints Church, Old Penshaw.

The Rectory, Penshaw, in the early 1900s. The Reverend F.G. Holme with family members.

Wedding of Joseph Turnbull and Margaret Britton at St Oswald's Church, Shiney Row in the early 1930s.

St Oswald's Church, Shiney Row, *circa* 1912. This brick-built church was erected in 1909-10 at a cost of £1,000.

St Oswald's Church, Shiney Row, *circa* 1920s. Note the tram lines.

The Parish Hall at Shiney Row in the early 1900s.

Shiney Row St Oswald's Mothers' Union Concert Party, *circa* 1926.

St Oswald's Church Youth Club, Shiney Row, *circa* 1924.

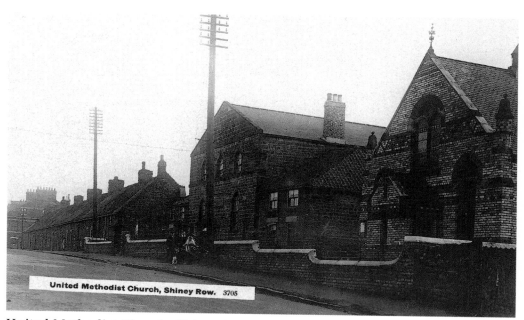

United Methodist Church, Shiney Row, *circa* 1900.

The Primitive Methodist Church, Shiney Row, *circa* 1906.

The Wesleyan Church, Penshaw Place, Shiney Row, *circa* 1908.

Members of the Methodist Church, Shiney Row, *circa* 1930s.

The Wesleyan Methodist Chapel at Junction Row, Shiney Row, was opened in March 1872 and closed its doors for the last time on 5th January 1958. It never exceeded 25 members in all of that time. For 57 years, George Dacres of Golf House, Jane Pit Cottage, was associated with the chapel and for the last 38 of those years he served as Sunday School Superintendent.

St Aidan's Church, Herrington in the early 1900s. St Aidan's was built in 1886 at a cost of £4,376. The Earl of Durham contributed £2,000 towards the cost and also gave the land for the site.

Michael Gardner and Barbara Watson's wedding group outside St Aidan's Church, Herrington, in the early 1920s.

Wesleyan Methodist Church, Newbottle, built 1786. Many of the people who attended this church were potters. It is now demolished.

Below: St Matthew's Church, Newbottle. The church building dates from 1886.

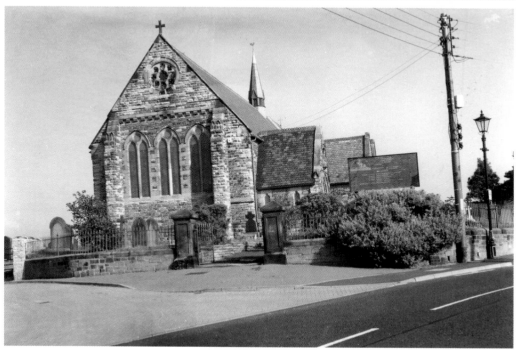

St Matthew's Church, Newbottle, *circa* 1918.

The Church and Rectory at Newbottle, *circa* 1913.

LEISURE

The Philadelphia Lodge Banner at the Durham Miners' Gala.

Cox Green Railway Station, *circa* 1960s. This station was a popular stopping off point for day-trippers from nearby towns and villages.

A 'family outing' through the woods at Cox Green in the early 1900s.

A trip from Sunderland District Tramways, Philadelphia depot, *circa* 1920s. Note the open-topped charabanc with a cover at the back to roll forward in case of inclement weather.

Lambton Engine Works electric shop trip, 10th June 1951.

Shiney Row Male Voice Choir in Trinity Methodist Church, Shiney Row, in 1979. The choir was formed in 1959. Fifth from the right in the front row is Fred Wilson (conductor), sixth from the right is Brian Thompson (president) and next to him is George Gent (pianist).

The Gem Cinema, New Penshaw, *circa* 1979. In 1921 William Henderson was manager of the Gem.

The Tivoli Cinema at Herrington Burn after it had closed its doors to the public. The manageress at the Tivoli in the 1920s was Lizzie Winsley.

Club Recreation Pavilion, New Herrington, *circa* 1908.

Youngsters involved in various activities at the YMCA, Herrington Burn, with some of their youth leaders.

Enjoying the 'Gala' atmosphere, these young people are from the YMCA, Herrington Burn.

Shiney Row Primary School parents and childrens walk to the Roman Wall in 1999.

Shiney Row Primary School visit to Patterdale in 1998.

Newbottle School netball team, 1951-52. Back row: M. Bewick, E. Smith, H. Reed and N. Robson. Front row: unknown, J. Knight, C. Ede, E. Wren and Mrs Blenkinsop.

Barnwell Primary School girls' netball team, 1955.

Barnwell Primary School boys' cricket team.

Philadelphia's Sunderland District Tramways football team, 1920-21.

Herrington School football team, local champions in 1933-34. Back row, left to right: C.L. Bassett (in charge of football), S. Armstrong, M. Batey, J. Addison, Mr Haver (headmaster), W. Collins, H. Cafferty and T. Hunt. Middle row: W. Bassert, T. Lilley, W. Tait (captain), R. Fisher and P. Groves. Front row: H. Clark, W. Chalmers, R. Henderson and T. Rose.

Shiney Row School football team with shield, 1930-31.

Shiney Row Senior School football team, 1964.

Shiney Row Junior School football team, 1965.

Shiney Row, St Oswald's football team, 1949-50. Included are: Ivan Lonsdale, Bill Edger, S. Bewick, H. Appleby, G. Lowery, G. Thompson, F. Smith, B. Fyfe, F. Hood and H. Brunton.

New Penshaw Football Club, 1941. Middle row, third from left is Thomas Curry. This was wartime and these men were mostly miners who also served in the Home Guard part-time.

Barnwell Primary School boys' football team with their cups and medals.

Saved! The boys of Newbottle School enjoy their outdoor exercise.

All smiles! The boys' football team of Our Lady Queen of Peace RC Primary School proudly hold their winning cups in 1979. Back row: Kevin Kerrigan, Patrick Cahill, David Forster, Kevin Murphy, Simon Doherty, David Blair and Mr F.C. Kerrigan. Front row: Peter Storey, Keith Bowman, Gerard Long, Dominic Curran, David Walker and Colin Neat.

The beginning of Shiney Row Lower School sports day, 1999.

Barnwell Primary
School Infants sports
day, 1989.

Hitting the heights.
Newbottle Primary
School physical
training lesson.

It is not easy – Newbottle Primary School's sports day in 1991.

This book would not be complete without one final look at Penshaw Monument – which stands proudly over the villages of Penshaw, Shiney Row, Philadelphia and Newbottle.

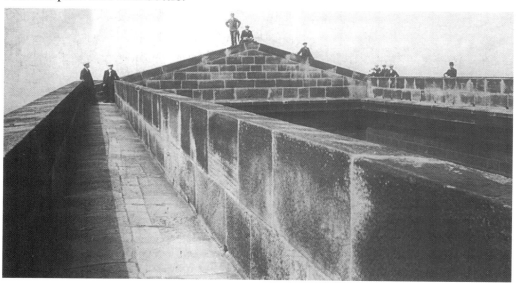

The People's History

To receive a catalogue of the latest titles send a large SAE to:

The People's History Ltd
Suite 1, Byron House
Seaham Grange Business Park
Seaham, County Durham
SR7 0PY